This book belongs to:

_____

_____

ISBN 978-1-990237-04-1

First published in 2022 by
Society for Behavior SciAnts, BC, V5H 1K6, Canada

Behavior SciAnts
Disseminating Behaviour Science

Going to
My New School

Written by Stephanie Chan

Illustrated by Citra Lani

I am _____. I am _____ years old.
I will go to _____ School in _____!
I will be in Grade _____.

This is the school. Everything is new for me.
In the morning, I will be here on time. "Ringggg!"

This is the entrance.

This is the office.
The principal is here.

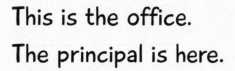

good
morning
_____!

This is the classroom.

At carpet time, I will sit nicely and listen.

At center time, I will share and take turns when playing with classmates.

When doing my table work, I will try my best.
It's OK to make mistakes. "Oops!"

For snacks and lunch,
I will eat healthy food.

This is the library.
I will read books, borrow books,
and listen to stories here.
I will be quiet. Shhh!

"Ringgg!" It's recess time!
I will play with my friends on the playground.
It will be fun!

It's time for music class! We will line up
and walk with marshmallow toes in the hallway.

In the music room, we will sing, dance, and play different musical instruments!

When it's gym time,
we will do exercise and play games.

When I feel I need
to go to the washroom,
I will raise my hand and tell the teacher.

After I use the washroom,
I will wash my hands.

When I don't understand something,
I can raise my hand and ask for help.
I will wait nicely for the teacher
to help me.

I will have new teachers and new friends.
They are nice!

Let's play!

I like my new teachers
and new friends.

I will listen to teachers,
and follow school rules.

When I listen to teachers and follow school rules...

everyone is happy.

Good job!

My teacher will praise me.

My friends will like playing with me.

Is this important to me and does it make me proud?

I am a big kid!

I will go to Grade _____ at _____ School.

I will meet new teachers and new friends there.

I will learn a lot, have fun, and do a good job!

What School Rules Should We Follow?

Parents, after reading the book with your child, please ask these questions to reinforce what they have learned.

What should we do...
- ✓ when we go to school in the morning?
- ✓ at carpet time?
- ✓ when playing with classmates at centre time?
- ✓ at table-work time?
- ✓ at snack or lunch time?
- ✓ in the library?
- ✓ in the gym?
- ✓ at recess time?
- ✓ when walking in the hallway?
- ✓ in music class?
- ✓ when we need to go to the washroom?
- ✓ when we need help?

I'm ready to go to the new school!

Now, let's make a visual schedule for my new school with the following pictures!

recess time 	**gym**	**carpet time**	**lunch** 
bathroom 	**arts and crafts** 	**center time** 	**music**
table time 	**snack** 	**going home** 	Scan code to receive the digital version of the schedule pictures. 

About the Author

Stephanie Chan, Ph.D.c., M.Ed., BCBA, is a researcher, author, early childhood educator, and behavior analyst. She published many children's books and educational materials primarily in the areas of perspective-taking, problem-solving, and understanding emotions and feelings. She also published scientific papers and presented in international conferences on various topics.

Stephanie lives in Vancouver, Canada, with her lovely family. She is the clinical director of a non-profit organization PlaySmart Child Development Society.

Made in United States
Troutdale, OR
08/26/2024

22336601R00021